...is for HOUSEWIVES!

Aa

...is for ANDY.
His cameras are
always close by.

Bb

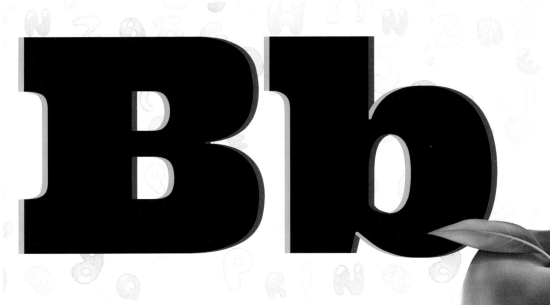

...is for BLOOP, which we all heard NENE cry.

Cc

...is for CHATEAU Sheree. Can you believe that it got completed?!

Dd

...is for DRAG me Monique. That argument was very heated.

Ee

...is for
EGGS a La Francaise,
the best meal to have
at the beach!

Ff

...is for the little FAMILY van. Boy, did that make Vicki Screech!

Hh

...is for HI GREEN. Most would know not to wear green to a wake.

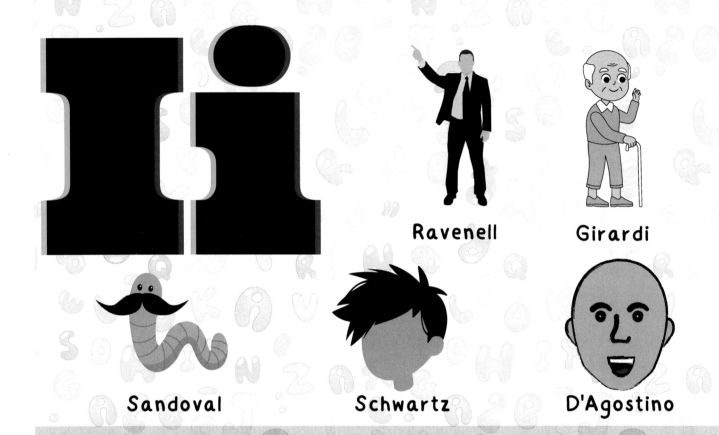

Ravenell

Girardi

Sandoval

Schwartz

D'Agostino

...is for IT'S about Tom, but now you have to ask which one.

Jj

...is for JOVANI.
Dorinda was truly
DONE!

Kk

...is for
KENYA Moore hair care,
the drumline was a site
to see!

L l

...is for LUCY LUCY Apple Juicy. LVP will not be having Dorit for high tea!

Mm

...is for the MORGAN letters, which you should never touch.

Nn

...is for the NOT a white refrigerator. That apartment was rough.

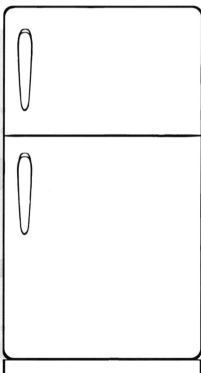

Oo

...is ON display, each and every day, every day, every day!

Pp

...is for POSCHE Fashion Show, where the ladies shashay.

Qq

...is for QUIET woman. Make sure you know which is your plate!

Rr

...is for the RUMORS, that these ladies often create.

Ss

HAMPTON
UNIVERSITY

...is for SING SING, always be careful with your hot box.

Tt

...is for TOM'S house was broken into and he confronted the burglar and then he had to go have eye surgery and then my son had to go over and help and then my son, he rolled over his car five times on the way home!

Uu

...is for UGLY leather pants!

Vv

...is for
VILLA Rosa!
It's so pretty, you might
think you are in France!

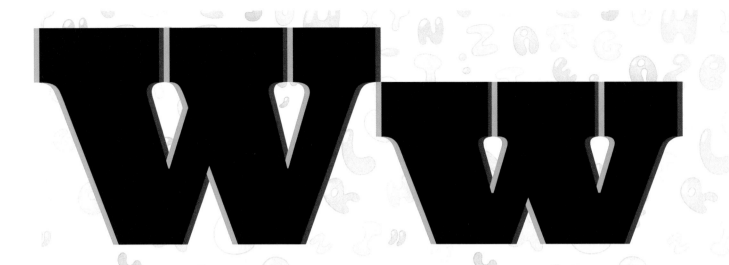

...is for
WOW BETHENNY WOW!
Women should always
support women!

WOW!

Xx

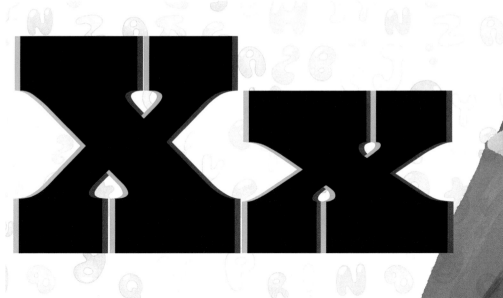

...is for X-FACTOR all the ladies have it and that's a fact!

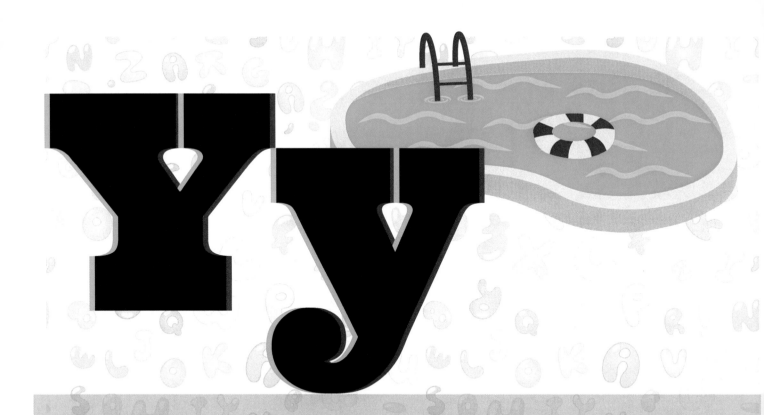

Yy

...is for YOUR husbands in the pool, so you better watch your back!

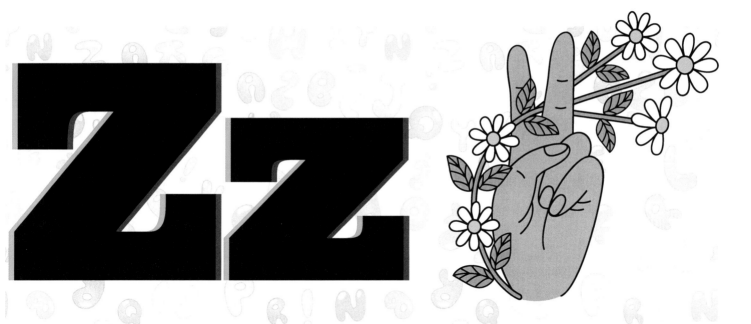

Zz

...is for ZEN WEN, who has four degrees. She believes you should always use BRAVO to remember your ABC's!

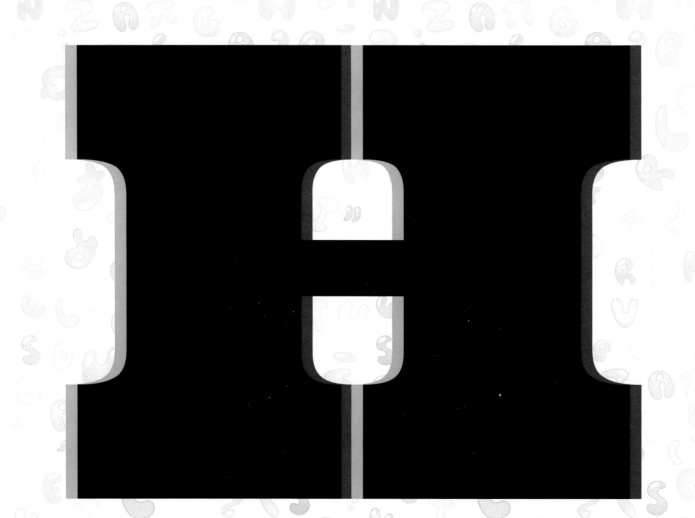

...is for HOUSEWIVES!

Made in United States
North Haven, CT
09 May 2024

52332175R00018